Doing *70*

Hettie Jones

Hanging Loose Press
Brooklyn, New York

Published by Hanging Loose Press, 231 Wyckoff Street, Brooklyn, New York 11217-2208. All rights reserved. No part of this book may be reproduced without the publisher's written permission, except for brief quotations in reviews.

www.hangingloosepress.com

Printed in the United States of America
10 9 8 7 6 5 4 3 2 1

Hanging Loose Press thanks the Literature Program of the New York State Council on the Arts for a grant in support of the publication of this book.

Cover painting by George Mingo (detail)
Cover design by Marie Carter

Some of these poems have appeared in *Café Review*, *Driftwood*, *For Four Hetties*, *Hanging Loose*, *Italics Mine*, *Present/Tense*, and *Wildflowers*.

Library of Congress Cataloging-in-Publication Data available on request.

ISBN: 978-1-931236-72-0 (paper)
ISBN: 978-1-931236-73-7 (cloth)

 Produced at The Print Center, Inc. 225 Varick St., New York, NY 10014, a non-profit facility for literary and arts-related publications. (212) 206-8465

for Kenneth Brown and for Guthrie Ramsey, Jr.

Contents

Doing 70

Raw Space

True Sisters

Our Lady of Perpetual Scaffolding

Doing
70

Weather

My folder of poems
labeled "weather" holds
no clues as to whether
or not there'll be any

weather to count on, say,
a hard rain like "little nails," or
that deluge "plunging radiant"

now that we've plunged into war
and wars don't stop like rain stops

like that last slow drizzle
onto the old tin bathroom vent

sweet hint of growth
in the soft wet drift north

fire or ice, fire or ice

are you breathing, are you lucky enough
to be breathing

Here Is

a woman who knows
what here is, through

long years of being
here

by a window that offers
others, there

here then is
this woman

ten thirty pm
on April seven

a struggling spring
in two thousand six

Living on Air

As a song is an air, a poem is

an unexpected catching
of breathtaking
life

And there's new proof – our feelings guide us!
How gracious of science
to let those of us with feelings
off the hook

so look—across the street
a narrow window has just now
filled with aqua light
                          —a southern sea!

in a hard won New York night

Snapshots

A Rogue's Gallery

the self-important
college girl
declines to return
my gaze

the teen
profiles
audacious
breasts

both in debt to
the four year old

blinded by sun and just then
coming upon a new
dimension, a third eye
to an inner space
that will save her for life

       —and from it—

it is huge in her
it will hold us all

and it is waiting
for her
to fill it

Long Time Gone

His face like a deck of cards
to a complicated game
of attitudes

Hers on a fast track to delusion:

Here's a woman who thinks she's
getting something

more than a reason to challenge
her failure at love. And she failed

but I am forgiven

Double Edges

Back

(1968)

Disorder, a discipline of loneliness,
Prose, but not poems and nothing at all
Low-down. How to dance alone
In front of a mirror or holding effigies.

Relics. Replicas. Imagination,
Wet or dry.   Cold.

Forth

(2002)

The assignment this week
is to breathe

all over the page, because

to breathe is to exist, derived from

"stand forth"

Day

The woman rising from my bed
puts her new foot into my old shoe

               strides out never thinking
               she'll go down like the rest

                            Night

                            lies in wait for the woman
                              who works days

                                    night begs
                        the question, then barricades
                          the restless doors

Muscular Crepuscular

folds this kitchen
　　into his dark arms

draws coverlets of silence
　　up the stairs

bides with me until I'm free
　　of everyday determination

and he is free to rise from me
　　to his next delicious conjugation

The Second Person, as in "Sometimes You Feel As If"

Surely you, the second person,
are having a few fabulous or even scandalous
       feelings I'd enjoy—

So how come I seldom use *you* to describe *me*?

Humility? Arrogance? Simple self-regard?

       Other possibilities come to mind
       and as usual I, not you, am guilty
       of all of them

       —though surely you do sometimes feel
        as if, as in woefully or joyfully
        first person singular—

I can't seem to come to any conclusions about this.

Still it's not like you've been in my room all night
begging a poem from it

I'm looking around and there's
no one here but me to win or lose

And the rest, with due respect, is all yours.

Plan

not the poem at the slippery tip of the tongue

or the one under the hand, that unripe, skintight tomato

but the poem asleep in the heart, the hardworking heart

    that runs the whole show so uncomplaining—

loose-lipped heart, openhanded heart

    heart that lays the pen down sated

"What I Think When I Ride the Train"

I'm in a subway
  under words

an image train
  on a sound track

a level below the
  tongue that twists

into lures like "effort"
  and "slouch"

Still, this must mean
when I ride the train
that I'm thinking we're all
in it

that's what I'd like
to think I'm thinking
when I ride the train

that we're in it
together, that

we're in this thing
together

Snow Job

Shoulder to shoulder, nearly snowed under,
the stone heads of the cemeteried dead
gaze at a low, forthright mountain's
flank. Bristle of black branches
stands of evergreen interwoven

Between the dead and the land, the living
dig themselves out, on roads
that repeat the mountain's curves

and where, in passing, I see both sides

    insistent life   implacable death

        first one, then the other

Fault Lines

Pride

only this
against power
and time

      under which
      we labor, held

            to marks we
            can't see

                        Fear

                        slick treasure,
                        confidante

                        storm my fingers,
                        my shaking heart

                        rise and pass

                        beloved antagonist,
                        rise and pass

North American Reciprocal Shimmering Heart

five words together by chance

word pie flung
in the face
of order

like keeping your cool
to stay hot—

in my North American Reciprocal
Shimmering Heart

I hold out hope

Ready or Not

for Alicia Loving Cortes

A friend, dying too soon, said
she wasn't afraid she just wasn't
ready

When I was five, a very old uncle said,
"It's enough already."

Even then I could not comprehend
leaving all the small, ironclad
eventualities

And now, way past midway,
I think I won't ever be ready

never ready, never
enough already

Doing 70: A Passion Play

for Helene Dorn 1927-2004

Act 1

On the Mass Pike, at the first rest stop past Boston,
the starter breaks. The lights and radio go on,
but there's no click click. It's six pm
on a hot, humid, summer Saturday.
I'm headed home to New York
with a file box of letters in the trunk.

What could have caused this?
Overheating? I'd only been doing seventy.

The cashier calls three times for a guy
who appears at last with doped-up eyes
and writes down a number.
The man on the phone says
Look for a truck, but it might take
twenty to thirty and if he doesn't come
call me back.

A pattern? A portent? Well,
a second chance.

I start right away for the car.
The box of letters is heavy every
way. Thirty pounds, four decades,
two women, one dead, the other
stuck. Fuck.

But even as the door of the store closes behind me
a flatbed roars into the sunburnt parking lot.
Waving and pointing, I run the rest of the way,
and soon

an audience has gathered, a three-generation family
with two awed children. Everyone likes a driver,
and here's a young, good-looking, acrobatic one,
who parks precisely, load-ready, then
in one quick movement swings out,
takes my keys, turns on the lights and radio, and says
it's probably the starter.

Well I know *that*.

But Ryan, as I'd know *him*, notes
at once that I've gone past cause to effect.
He tells me the terms, admits he's been
to New York twice, though not in many years.
(How many years are in him, maybe
twenty-three?) But his self-possession rivals
his grace. I assure him I know the roads.
When we agree, his excitement
parallels my relief.   He loads the car
on the bed and me in the cab.
The family watching waves
as we drive away.

This is when I discover that the truck has no a/c
and not too many shocks.

Windows down, we leave the Pike for local roads.
Ryan stays on his phone, all about getting lucky
and going to New York City. At a station he gets
diesel, cash, a big jug of water.

Back on the highway,
the shouting wind is a third rider.

On my mind and in the side mirror
the car on the flatbed, all those old words
stirring. It's the night of a huge blue moon
as July becomes August, and I've been doing seventy
for sixteen days and I'm still new to it.
A broken starter isn't auspicious.
And you, Helene, are not even here
for the humor. Shit.

But so far, nothing has changed about
being here now to get there then. It got us
on this truck. What I have of you is safe
in the trunk. And I'm in the cab
with Ryan. When I ask if he minds
if I take off my shoes, he says
do what you like
we've got a long way to go.

But of course we haven't gone far
before I'm in love. Every time
we hit rough road the glove compartment
falls open into my lap, and my bare foot
closing it seems
provocative

though I know doing seventy means
giving up the pretty boys

you lust you lose, you hear
the cry of the crows

Act 3

It's hard to talk over the wind.
Sometimes we travel miles between sentences.
The Red Sox have just made a terrible trade.
Ryan goes to college on and off for law
enforcement. He's two months into
driving this truck. One time,
in Jamaica Plain, a guy
who couldn't pay tried to
stab him.

At the midway stop, he asks me
where we are on the map.
Like me he likes to learn the road.
Then he helps me get a drink.
We are to each other a profile only,
yet there's easy body language
between us, some physical trust. I'm sweaty
and dirty and beginning to feel as if
I'm the one who really got lucky.

After the Pike we take 84 to 91 to 95,
Ryan reporting to his dispatcher,
whose staticky voice seems tense,
as if her tracking might not prevent
his transfiguring. But despite a side trip
over the Triboro to Queens (my fault),

he gets us into Manhattan and onto
Second Avenue, where the real fun begins:

It's Saturday night, New York!
The neighbors are out! There are buses, taxis,
bikers, bad drivers, jay walkers,
cell phone talkers, a jabber and clank
            of outdoor eaters—

Ryan drives among them all, Second Avenue
end to end.

Act 4

At the parking lot he once again
commands an audience. After driving
one hundred ninety miles at night on
four unfamiliar major highways
he backs his load through tight,
curving, graveled spaces, then
slides it gently into place.

Ryan's next feat is to perfectly parallel park
a flatbed on a New York City street,
where he gets the credit form signed
in all the right places, and then, ready
to turn back, guns the truck
across a double yellow, yelling,
"What the hell, I'm from Worcester,
 and I'll just make a U-ie here!"

30

Reprise

The box is nestled in my hall
the route I've written out reviewed
and Ryan reminded that he said
he'd take a nap. By now it's eleven,
he won't get back till four. But no,
he'll blast the radio, work
the overnight, why not. He knows
what holds him, lucky Ryan,
who drove to New York City,

and lucky us, my dear Helene,
the dead and living
safely home.

Raw Space

Raw Space: 9/11/01

That's what it's like, I think, raw space.

Our nerves rubbed raw. Exposed.

Like the fruits of the earth we eat raw, we feel devoured.

Look up raw, I write. Look up space.

Look at the poem left raw.

Learn to live in a raw space.

Genuflection to Petty Officer First Class Leonette Masters

shown in a photo
with her mother and daughter
before her departure
for needless war

needless death was in the photo too
until it got cropped

but I know it's there
just as I know from the caption that
Leonette Masters' daughter is three

and though I don't know her mother's age
or hers, I know how their drawn-down mouths
hold a strangle of unshed tears

each time I look it's as though
I'd never seen them before, or imagined
a dock full of people
looking at needless death edging
closer and closer into the frame until it
obliterates this picture

Preservation

The author:
known only as Debora
fought and died with the Underground
in Warsaw, 1944

Her diary:
twenty torn, burned, fused-together
pages the size of playing cards
written in secret, stashed, and
as she had instructed

Retrieved:
from behind a radiator
in the ruins of Resistance headquarters
1945

By her friend, Lusia,
who held it sixty years, then
dying instructed: restore
and share

Some words from a preliminary translation:

bombs   fire   angels   Nazis

mother's coffin   a pile of corpses

ghetto is a certain death

7/13/03   Gifts

for Susan Maldovan

The first from Kamer,
a women's group in Turkey

to Cemse Allak, who had not died
though the side of her head
had been, repeatedly, struck.

Thirty-five and single, she'd been stoned
—and then abandoned—for having sex
or being raped, same shame.

In the hospital where Cemse lay, paralyzed
and mute, the women of Kamer said,
 "If you hear us, blink." For three months
they held her hands while she spoke to them
with her eyes. And then she died.

Against custom, risking their lives,
they carried her coffin to the graveyard.
Women in jeans, t-shirts, shades.

Here for them is my all-day robin
—appearing, disappearing, reappearing—

> the 4th St. water tower song
> the 5th St. senior citizens center song
> and the song of the 6th St. tenement's
> open roof door

in memory of Cemse Allak
gone like birdsong
in the blink of an eye
in the casting of the first stone

At Writing, at Taconic Correctional

dilapidated trailer

fluorescent hum

our breath over the light's *ohm*

on the fake wood wall an elephant
gazes from a sun-drenched haven

to here, no haven,
no heaven. Nevertheless

this moment:
the place that's always
home.

About Face

8/6/02

In Ghana, in August, in
the Golden Tulip's
Demba Lounge

Nat Cole sings
"Merry Christmas"

as lone white men
on cell phones listen,
some with evident
nostalgia, to a black man
singing of home

Father Carney Still Makes the *Times*

for James Carney, who died in Honduras

1983

Father Carney, you'll be pleased to know
your death in the jungle of Olancho
has made page four

where all around you ads for clothes
compete for our attention

Oh they're class ads, Father Carney,
Barneys, Saks Fifth, Lord & Taylor too

Though not the Lord you served so well
they killed you for it, Father Carney

2003

Hang on Father Carney, they're out there
looking for your bones. Hang on even if the worms

have long since claimed your flesh. They'll know you

by the bullet holes, and those for whom you died
and near whom you'll be found, yes Father Carney

you will certainly be found

Air Jamaica

Good Friday, 2000

Beyond the bougainvillea-covered chain link
        binding me into this hotel lobby's
           legacy of mildew and tropical sorrow

Gina   holds down her chicken shack

       in dust that masks the sea
          that bore in Europe's lust

Oh Jesus, I'm checked in and choked off
       and it's me and Gina
         in Kingston

         in our inherited
         dilemma

Perks

perquisite—perk for short—starts at the Latin *perquisitus*
"to have searched everywhere, inquired diligently"

then goes perking along to the Middle English
perquisitum, what the privileged expected
as their due, so I guess they found
what they were looking for

because—*quelle surprise !*—perk arrives at
how they control today, with unexpected extras
(after a long, diligent, underprivileged search)

as, it was a perk to live in France
rent free for a month, *ca ne mange pas de pain*
as they say there, it didn't eat a lot of bread
even where there's a lot of bread to be eaten

not like here, where we earn and spend
our dough, rolling out newly inflated
images of Thomas and George and Andrew

praying for our daily while
knowing there's no living
on *pain* alone, so we continue to search everywhere,
inquiring with diligence, looking
for bread but asking
for roses

Shadows Matter

today every pigeon
had one
and passing cars
pulled some

and in the classroom
my past was a long shadow
over my students'
sweet attention

and don't the shadows of mis-
interpretation
lurk in the complicated pattern
of our national carpet, oh

America, what if we lose the
little we've gained, our human
failing

and beginning again, our
pitiful attempt
at a body politic

in the ever-shifting shadows
coming then
going

Word

What's the good one

Whassup
            with the word
the good word everyone
wants to hear

Word up?

                    Is it
this we're asking now

one good word to take us
from those we fear

Gear

from a ratchety wheel
to the stuff we haul

armies in high gear   or
from the outset she was geared toward teaching
but later dismayed to find she'd become a cog

oh cogs of the world, unite
behind your best definition:

in carpentry you are the tongue in one timber
fitting the corresponding slot in another

let us, then, gear up

Rabbits Rabbits Rabbits

2/1/87—5/1/05

The summer before that Year
of the Rabbit

someone painted rabbits
on the sidewalk. Two
I saw at once, hoped
for the third and there
it was, yes—right
in front of the house, oh

Rabbits Rabbits Rabbits

Overlooked thereafter, snow-
covered, downtrodden

Until one morning
under my shovel, the paint
still clear, it appeared

the third Rabbit—
                    Indelible

another snow that night
it was gone again next morning
I thought of it there
waiting it out

ready to run
ready to come
into its own again

Don't leave your loose ends
lying around in America.

Don't miss your entrée
into universal weather.

But don't count on easy.

That's a certainty, brothers and sisters,
don't count on easy.

True Sisters

For Arlene Tyson at 93 Years

You keep things, don't you
she said   when she saw
the scarf she'd bought me
                    years before

You can wear red, she said

Red things I keep:
the hat to that scarf
my half gloves for the house
my hidden heart

ink ink ink

Double-Decker

Moms

First

Volunteered for World War II. In her Gray Lady
uniform, gray from headdress to shoe, she wore
the dignity, stature, and strangeness of the nun,
the drama of the nurse, the exquisite, hidden adult
world. She worked, she was skilled, she won the war.

Second

the day she died
the blue jay in my bedroom

  like my grief
      stunned
    wall to wall

Kids

Blooms

My daughter
has brought me
ten
perfect
yellow
tulips

It might
as well
be spring.

Verbs

Listen, this one is good, she says:

The subjunctive is
the hypothetical future
of the past.

Indeed it is, I say:

Had you not been mine
I would be sad.
Because you are,
I'm glad.

Aunt Cora

for Cora Coleman 1927–2004

Aunt Cora joined the army,
found a girlfriend, left
the former and kept the latter
for thirty years. Aunt Cora,
as a court reporter, saw a
lot of undercover and over-
heard a lot more. Aunt Cora's
lover was a beauty
and they lived happily
until they didn't. We loved our Cora's
wayward ways, her forward march, the way
she kept us all in step. Altogether, we loved
Aunt Cora. All together: We Loved Aunt Cora!

For Margaret of Sixth Street

who is probably dead, RIP

Whenever I met Margaret
the rest of the day was magic

Margaret might have been ninety-some,
she never would say. One day

after years of meeting her
on the street

I took the plunge
and kissed her cheek

then watched her grin
around her three
remaining teeth.

Six Ways of Looking at Loss

Just before I lost my mother's pin
I lied about her. By the time
I told the truth
the deed was done.

Years ago, my mother was robbed.
Only this pin and two earrings
were left.

Is that a Miro, asked the woman.
No, it's my mother's, I said.
I like to wear it, though I'm
not sure she liked me.

Here is a silver pin
with blue stones.
Someone is picking it up and
taking it home.

What a beautiful pin, she says
as he fastens it to her breast and
takes her into his arms. The pin
is large and heavy between them.

My mother turns, her body
is air, her love for me
gone in silver, gone in blue stones.

Free Wheeling

for Zoe Margaret Hettie Chapman Brown, b. 2/13/05

Oh, now I can drive to Brooklyn, to Brooklyn
over the bridge. I can drive the lengthy avenues

the route in my head
and my eyes on the road

and a heart for my girl and her guy
at the end

And then I can drive to Harlem, to Harlem's uptown air
to eyeball the rivers and ogle the skylines

and hug my dear girl and the sweet man she chose

and the new girl they've made as she grows
and grows

Finding the Photo and Giving Away the Jacket

It's so Forties, so smock, so
black wool with
a Peter Pan collar

a wide pleated back
and narrow loops
to rein it in
with something thin

I'm giving it to a girl
whose shoulders slope to
a slender waist

jet buttons to shine her up
bound buttonholes to keep her
from raveling

If she's reading this here are clues:
a famous long-dead designer's label
a sturdy silk lining, and

you don't want anything
underneath

It came from Domsey's
Warehouse, where the object
was to spend the day
with what was passé
until you got hold of it

I seldom wore that jacket
but did for one photo that's me
in the middle looking
all buttoned up

Though it fit perfectly
on my mother's rounded
red plastic hanger

it needed a pillbox
hat and high heeled
baby doll toes, neither of which
I needed

So girls—
if I couldn't
swing that wide back
into something freer

—something giving as well as fine—

surely one of you can.
And here it comes.

True Sisters, or *Caritas*

for PhDiva Kellie Jones

1.

In 1846, the United Order of True Sisters
started health and social services
for the needy of their sex

America's oldest women's
charitable organization,
they began on the Lower East Side,
at 56 Chrystie, which was then a synagogue,
where the Sisters were a secret order, steeped
in ritual and secret to spare the needy
the humility of charity

2.

In the ear's heart I carry
where lives what language
I learned on, the words "True Sisters"
are paired
    —and if I could not then
        comprehend *caritas*,
        I clearly heard its *gravitas*—

Yet absent facts—was the speaker, my mother,
a True Sister, with whom was she speaking,
and what would they have said,
across the river in Brooklyn?

And why, before I ever traced the Sisters
to it, have I always been drawn
to the building at 56 Chrystie ?

Something is there that I know
I'm supposed to remember

and if I could, I think I might
trace myself, too, but I know

that I can't, and that this loss
is less than the words, "True Sisters"
truly remembered, that *caritas*

3.

In 1919, the year the Infants Home of Brooklyn was established,
my mother, seventeen and a bookkeeper, was just out of
Bay Ridge High. In '24 she attended the dedication
of the Home's new building on 56th Street.

The button to prove this she saved all her life, a plain truth
among her costume jewels.

4.

In Berkeley, California, during the First World War,
the Phyllis Wheatley Club also started social service
projects. Its ten original members spent time
knitting socks for soldiers.

In 1914, Hettie Blonde Tilgheman took Phyllis Wheatley
over. Hettie ran her family's printing business, as well as
a lot of community business. When, in nearby Oakland,
some women founded the Fannie Wall Home for Colored
Orphans, the Wheatley Club made the Home its special project.

5.

Absent facts one links True Sisters as one chooses:

In '34, my mother named her second daughter Hettie

That year, despite the Great Depression, the Infants Home
of Brooklyn provided residential care for forty-two
dependent orphans, and the Wheatley Club
kept up its payments to the Fannie Wall Home
                for Colored Orphans

        which today continues as a day care center
        operated by the City of Oakland, as
        the Infants Home of Brooklyn harbors
                disabled children

And thus I rest my case, True Sisters chosen

Women in Black

A vigil at sundown, Beijing, 1995

Patterns in the dust of
different kinds of shoe soles
               Black on black
we sway like grain, like the woman
beside me, the scar of the burning
she escaped

              When she turns to me,
smiling, the scar is a path, slick
in the gathering dark   Half the world
          is ours to take

Naming Hettie Slocum

Hettie Slocum once went
halfway around the world and back
in a sailboat. Then she gave up
the nautical life for good
and took off to farm

leaving her husband, Captain Joshua,
the well-known navigator-storyteller,
to the heave and swell of that vast
and wily mother, the sea.

Hettie was a pretty seamstress,
twenty-four and fresh from Nova Scotia;
Slocum, a cousin, forty-two and lonely.
His first wife, love of his life, mother
of his sons, had died.   It was 1886.

Hettie was game; she sewed Slocum's sails
cruised with him and the boys
to Rio, bought a tall hat, survived
an epidemic. He wrote a book
about their adventures, called her

his wife, called her "brave enough to face
the worst storms"—but never once mentioned
her name. Let us then remember her: Hettie!
        Hettie Slocum!

Now all is said and done.

"Starting Here, What Do You Want to Remember?"

1.

I want to remember the noise
of the nights I've forgotten

like this high-pitched plaint
from a young woman, passing

I want to remember I
heard her

Listening, we can lean to starboard
or port. Me in this chair I can

go either way. What days
I've heard.

I want to remember
I listened.

2.

I want to remember the rape
of the already mutilated
circumcised Darfur women

raped by custom, raped
to control, raped to death

oh, if I could, in the same breath
reveal their pain and
relieve them of it

Saida Abdukarim was working
in her vegetable garden when
three men seized her, saying
"You're black, so we can,"
then raped her and beat her
with sticks and guns

though she was eight months
pregnant

At first too hurt to walk
two weeks later she had
not, so far,
miscarried

I want to remember
her unending withstanding
this endless miscarriage
of justice

3.

I want to remember the students
bursting out Apex Technical

a girl rubbing a boy's back and he
groaning and folding in half

real pleasure passing as pretend

I want to remember the girl
looking up, catching my grin

and returning, unrestrained,
a smile so full of light

I rode its dazzle all through Chelsea

bearing this witness with
the open eye I want
to remember

Our Lady of Perpetual Scaffolding

Our Lady of Perpetual Scaffolding

1.

Midnight blue lady
steel-legged, sign-covered
every shred an artful
dangle—like Herrick's
errant lace, oh

Lady, save us from those who
would that these old bricks fly

their own high the only righteous

us out of sight and in the dark

confined—yet in debt—oh Lady,
to your blue and most beneficient
verandah

2.

Forest green Lady harbors
dis-
carded
Christmas tree

3.

One fine round red Lady!
a full red skirt—a tutu—

on a brick red
building

4.

in passing, note
this Lady's ragged
razor wire
tiara

5.

Fell
from a tenth floor
over Times Square

a young woman, onto
Our Lady of the
Second Story Scaffolding

Nineteen
a winter coat
a red bandanna

suspected of stealing
tried instead to get
away, tried
the elevator, the stairs
tried a window

onto a ledge
and trying to grab a billboard
lost her balance

plunged eight floors
onto you, Our Lady of the
Second Story Scaffolding

your open arms the last
she ever knew

Genuflections to the Cable Guys from Time Warner

Genuflection on the rainy street
to the cable guys
from Time Warner

whose blueprint shows
on the roof above us
        a cable box
                        which I know does not
                        off their damp paper exist

                        and they know they need
                        to see for themselves
            but the way is barred
            by an undersized, overdressed
            older white woman
            in raveling fingerless gloves

Genuflection in the hall
to the cable guys
from Time Warner

so young, so wet, and oh so sour
when I ask for free cable for taking them up

Genuflection in the house
to the cable guys
from Time Warner

who find nothing on the roof

and are laughing coming down

the one who says, oh, you have a nice apartment
and the one who reaches to shake my half-gloved hand

sweet meeting, these bare, wet fingers

Walking Billboard Boulevard

The boards at Astor Hole were new
and blue, and offered words as well as
windows onto
earth and brick and stone
too soon reburied

Then suddenly the boards were green
with spots of blue
and spotted too with signs
instructing "Post No Bills,"
which were bills themselves—
oh language!

holding even when the bills—

      that spread the word
      gave voice
      gave tongue!—

when even they were gone

Jazz

for Hayes Greenfield

Hayes plays Teddy's on Wednesdays
but when Hayes plays sax out his third floor window
for me on the street on a rainy Monday

and the last soft notes Hayes plays drift down
ordained as rain, and as intended—

on this necessary pleasure, I fly—
from under my red umbrella

from my practices, my plodding certainties
from each of my accepted cares

into music, that pure and universal air

My Neighbor the Actor

for Michael Moran, 1944-2003.

Dear Mike,

There's an exercise for writing students
called "Letters That Can't Be Mailed,"
which is useful to encourage the exploration
of emotions or attachments, that kind of
"telling what's on your mind" thing,
and since I've always liked the idea
 I've written a few of these myself—

Well anyway, Mike, I know you're dying to hear
what I have to tell you—But oh no, you're not
dying to hear it, you *have* died and I forgot
we're not sitting on a sunny stoop on 5th Street
waiting for the parking regulations to go off,
and it isn't summer going into fall but a hard winter
of discontent and now disbelief that you're gone,
though all those trillions of atoms you possessed
in your big agglomerate Mikeness have gone *somewhere*—
we know this, it's science—

SoI have some idea you'll get this letter
even though I can't hand it over
on one of those interminable lines
at Cooper Station—

But there we are—*interminable*, see? Our feelings
show us how to think, the very word reinforces
what I've said, that you're somewhere,
never-ending like those lines at the Post Office,

so we don't have to lose you, why right this minute
in my mind's eye you're hurrying up 5th Street,
dressed for one audition or another, and you're calling out
to me like you always did, so I guess I'll answer
like I always did, and I suspect we'll all be
writing you from time to time, dear Mike, even though
we can't drop our letters in the slot—

So this is from me to you, Michael Moran
in the universe, to let you know, with much love,
that on the occasion of your passing, alternate side
parking was entirely—citywide—*suspended!*

Best Bets

Win

Halfway down the block
        some need tore into me

that afternoon, this familiar street

the thin logic of dream
the plain sight of my life
        since then

        Place

        where elevated railroads clattered

        where tall oaks now shade Peter Cooper's
            placid face

                and you can touch a lectern
                touched by Lincoln—!

        six new saplings
        in blossom, and a hard rain

Show

to intertwine
remarkable fingers
and thumbs

to see how handily the hand
comes into play, to
play it as it lays, hands
off or hands on

Shades

black for the season
blue for oh how I need

this gray afternoon
when the drummer at the green
subway kiosk
is
red hot

Praise

for Marie Ponsot

All praise the midweek market,
the first-of-the-season sexy zucchinis
gazing up from their crowded
boxes

All praise the cherries, their tight
red bellies, the sweet, slender stems
and the pit, ah the pit, to be nursed
in the mouth, cajoled to give up
its last sweet hold, praise

them. Praise all. All praise.

Renovation Reactivations

1. *That's my pail—*

not just the pail
but the dreams in
which it figures

the heater on which it sat
full of the water it gave to the
air of that room, with its dark
floors and crumbling brick walls

where I slept on a low bed
encaged, in order to
set the rabbit free

and one night was discovered
accompanied and uncovered

All this in a pail, all this water
under the bridge

2. *Old Tub Ode*

Old Tub, let me thank you
for Vinnie and Michael
of All County Sewer
who came with their snake
when the washing machine
was draining into you, and you—
          in protest I guessed—
wouldn't drain at all.

Vinnie and Michael seemed
shy when asked their names
as if they found it awkward
to be themselves into my ears.

Until they saw your curved lip
and claw feet and Michael yelled
and Vinnie laughed
and the snake brought up
clogged hair that wasn't
even mine, from your secret life

Old Tub. But thanks
for Vinnie and Michael,
whosever hair it was

3. *Retooling*

abandoned, a dozen years ago,
askew on a garbage can

a wooden toolbox
three feet long, a foot wide
  a hand's depth

designed—no, devised—

removable, adjustable, dividers
        and covers
soft rope handles with wax-dipped
     rolled ends, knotted
through drilled holes and rings

the wood like honey
the whole thing smooth as silk

form following function followed by
humble pleasure in contemplation:

hand tools at hand

I brought it home and put it to work.

        *

lidless, fabric-lined
retrofitted? aged?

hand tools at hand
the toolbox now holds books

4. *New Set Up*

Back in the day, from a catalog,
I bought a set of six paper clips

Yellow wire with a nice twist
set into molded plastic tops—
    skillfully fabricated, craftily affixed

      purple flower,
            yellow star, blue fish, red apple
                orange bicycle

                  —each its nature revealed

The sixth in the set was a heart, which I lost
one night I wore it carelessly
on my work, when I was in love
or more likely lust, but
        I missed it

and had to learn to trick words like
        lost heart

Now I've lined up the other five clips
on a card.
           The flower and the bike
are at each end and between them the star,
the fish and the apple. Everything they tell me
is true, for example that a fish out of water
can ride a bike in the Apple. As for losing heart—

no room on the card, no place in the lineup

5. *Plus ca change. . .*

the revamped vent speaks rain

old hand
new drum

Notes

p.6: "Little nails" is from Lonny Kaneko and "plunge radiant" from Denise Levertov.

p.16: This title is borrowed from Lucille Clifton.

p. 31: The diary was given to the Holocaust Museum in New York. I found the information in an article in *The New York Times*.

p. 32: Expelled from Honduras after eighteen years ministering to the poor, the Reverend James Carney, an American Jesuit, joined a group of rebels, along with whom he was captured and executed in 1983. Recently, skulls with bullet holes were uncovered in Olancho, and though none was Father Carney's, the search for him continues.

pp. 38 and 39: Saying "Rabbits Rabbits Rabbits" or something similar on the first day of the month, before one says anything else, has been called an "ancient and thoroughly English conceit," (*New York Times* Op-Ed article by Simon Winchester, October 7, 2006), one that has been practiced for many centuries, though apparently the first O.E.D. citation did not appear until 1920.

p. 52: Women in Black is an international organization. This action occurred at the First International Conference on Women in Beijing, 1995.

p. 54: This title is the taken from the first line of "You Reading This, Be Ready," by William Stafford (1914-1993).